ordinary sparkling moments

The Art of Finding Yourself

Christine MASON Miller * * *

2nd Edition
edited & revised

in an open place with light and air,

Lawrence

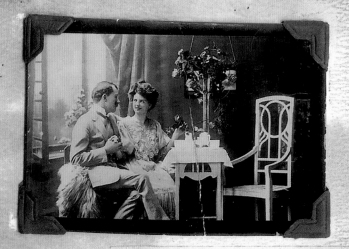

Who is John Galt?

Introduction

I wrote and published the first edition of *Ordinary Sparkling Moments* in 2008. I created written and visual content, scanned all the pages, formatted everything for my printer and, when the books were delivered to my doorstep (all 2200 of them), I was then faced with a long list of sales and distribution-related tasks in order to get those books into the hands of readers. I did it without the aid of an editor, art director or publisher, without anything like Kickstarter, which wouldn't launch for another year, and without a publicist or agent. I did it with the support of my husband and family, the encouragement of my friends and a belief in the notion that getting the book out into the world on my own terms would make a heck of a great story - a story that would inspire others to follow their own crazy dreams. It was a labor of love, an offering to my community and an example of possibility and passion. The first time I held it in my hands, it was as if my rib cage had been pried open, and the entire world could see my heart beating. I felt exposed and outrageous, vulnerable yet fearless. It was one of the most beautiful moments of my life.

When the opportunity came for a second edition, the first thing I did was re-read the book. I hadn't spent much time with it in a while, and my initial reaction was to start making notes about all the pages and passages I believed needed revising. My writing has improved! I've learned so much more! I have new experiences to share! Thinking how great it would be to change the original *Ordinary Sparkling Moments* into a "new and improved" version, I pulled out my crate full of all the 8.5" x 11" panels that made up the individual pages of the book to determine how difficult it would be to alter the mixed media collages for the new version.

The answer: not impossible, but far from straightforward.

Which got me thinking - did I ever intend for *Ordinary Sparkling Moments* to be a collection of perfectly constructed pieces of writing? Was I doing my best to honor the intentions and spirit behind the book by trying to insert new "reflections on success and contentment" that have been gleaned since it was first published? What was my motivation behind wanting to make it "better"? As I did the work to re-create a few pages and pare down the book to fewer pages, as per my publisher's request, I finally understood what *Ordinary Sparkling Moments* was about. I thought I knew back in 2008, but there was more to discover - insights I would not have stumbled upon had my publisher not provided me with the opportunity to breathe new life into the book.

Ordinary Sparkling Moments is a time capsule; it is a three-dimensional, full-color expression of the first moments I started considering myself a Writer with a capital W. It was my way to share the story of how I got there - how I made a big dream real, lost almost everything and then re-built my life with entirely new priorities. It was a 164-page symbol of the leap I was taking from all the comfortable spaces I'd inhabited not just as an artist, but as a creative, passionate woman determined to live a life of meaning, purpose and honesty. I wasn't the greatest writer in the world and I still had much to learn, but *Ordinary Sparkling Moments* celebrated that wobbly, vulnerable space between who I had been and who I had yet to be.

I've revised a number of pages, replaced a few and removed a few more, but it is the same book. Any edits were done to better express the point of each original passage rather than add new details or "update" them. I hope that even if you read the first edition, you make new discoveries in the second edition without getting the impression I've tried to turn it into a book that represents who I am *today*. I never set out to create a "perfect book" back in 2008, which is a great thing considering I misspelled the word "foreword" on *the cover of the book*, but it was in all the imperfections that the book was true to its intentions. *Ordinary Sparkling Moments* is a story about life, which can be confusing and nutty and full of surprises, but, in the end, is wondrously, kaleidoscopically beautiful in its own extraordinary way.

Fall 2014
Santa Barbara, California

All my Life I wanted to Be an artist, but I was never quite sure what that would Look Like. I did not imagine any specifics, it was simply Be an ARTist.

* * *

In 1993, my college roommate Elyse sent me *The Creative Companion*, the first book by author and artist SARK. I began reading the instant I pulled it out of the envelope and within an hour I knew what I wanted to do with my life. I wanted to be an artist and inspire the world to make their dreams real, just as SARK was doing for me *in that moment*.

A little over two years later, I began the journey of being an artist, making dreams real and inspiring others to do the same. My goals were grand and my determination unstoppable; I forged ahead believing there was no reason why I couldn't do exactly what I wanted to do. The dream I unfurled that year was called Swirly.

Swirly began in 1995 in a 10' x 10' spare room in my apartment as a line of handmade greeting cards. Over the next six years, it grew to an internationally recognized brand with oodles of Swirly stationery and gift products, an inspirational gift book translated in three languages, an 1100 square foot studio, and a ten pound portfolio. Swirly could be found in Barnes & Noble and Michael's Craft Stores, in catalogs and trade magazines, and in more than 1000 independent card and gift shops. In one especially rewarding project, Swirly designs were even licensed to the Girl Scouts of America. With the arrival of spring in 2001, the business was booming and expanding in directions I imagined would reward me with point-of-purchase displays at Target and a guest spot on the Oprah Winfrey show.

Something else happened in the spring of 2001:
my personal Life Completely Collapsed.

It is a long story, with episodes involving divorce, cancer, tumors, death, broken homes, multiple moves, anger, heartache, and loss. Tremendous loss. At one point I was laughing with a friend, positing the idea of taking the story I was currently living to a B-movie director whose films were only shown after midnight on cable TV and being rejected on the grounds that it was too melodramatic and outrageous to be believable.

There are some times in life when the only way to to cope is through laughter. During that ridiculously heartbreaking year, I laughed a lot, and that laughter saved me.

By the end of that year my lofty dreams for Swirly were replaced with longings of a different nature – a home of my own, miracle cancer cures and time with my friends and family. Suddenly, ideas I'd been holding onto for years – what I believed was my mission in the world – became much less important and, in some ways, positively unattractive. I emerged from those experiences questioning *everything* and, surprisingly, feeling restricted by the Swirly persona I'd invested so much in, realizing my work as an artist, woman, friend, daughter and partner encompassed much more. On the first day of 2002 I found myself on a very different path than the one I was on just one year earlier - one with an entirely new set of priorities and a deeper understanding of my own self.

Although Swirly continued to encourage dreamers around the world to follow their hearts, and will always be an important part of my identity, I have since shed much of my Swirly skin. As difficult as that process has been, it was necessary to let go of the dream I carried with me for so much of my life in order to see all the greater possibilities that existed beyond that world. During this metamorphosis, I realized living an authentic life rooted in honesty was more important than building a commercially successful brand, and that while they need not be mutually exclusive, it was imperative my work as an artist, writer or otherwise keep those two in alignment.

Through all the tumult, sadness and aftermath, I decided success was not about profit and loss statements and fulfillment didn't involve product placement. "Life's work" became less about fame or expertise and my most meaningful ambitions turned inward. I learned most dreams are not as unattainable as they might seem, but rarely grant permanent feelings of security, certainty or immortality. My search for things like contentment and inner peace began to narrow – towards my heart, my spirit and moments I was able to be totally and completely present, drowning in appreciation for whatever they had to offer me. And I stumbled upon a Truth that hasn't failed me since, which is that every moment, no matter how dire it appears, has something beautiful wrapped inside.

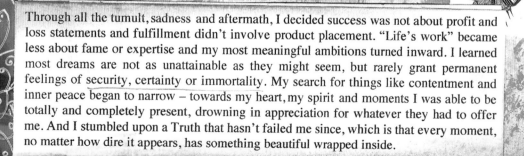

EVERY. SINGLE. MOMENT.

7

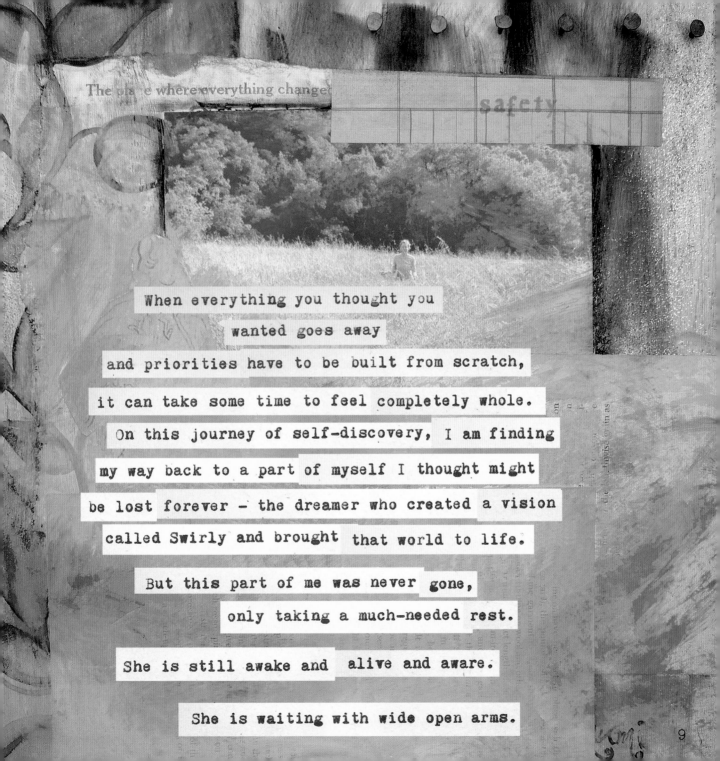

The place where everything changed   safety

When everything you thought you
wanted goes away

and priorities have to be built from scratch,

it can take some time to feel completely whole.

On this journey of self-discovery, I am finding

my way back to a part of myself I thought might

be lost forever - the dreamer who created a vision

called Swirly and brought that world to life.

But this part of me was never gone,

only taking a much-needed rest.

She is still awake and alive and aware.

She is waiting with wide open arms.

MY desire to share The Things I Do in a way that expresses their interconnectedness is not about wanting to put forth an ideal, glamorized version of my life. If anything, I am trying to convey something more down to earth, something that tells the story of an ordinary life filled with the spectrum of ordinary human experiences, all tied together by the desire to live a creative, meaningful life.

My day-to-day life is comprised of many things: I am an artist, writer, wife, stepmom, traveler, organizer, dog walker, runner, cyclist, and philosopher. I am not especially confident in the kitchen, get distracted easily, have bouts of overwhelming insecurity, and love the smell of celery. In all of this, I strive to keep everything in alignment with integrity, courage, and compassion. No matter how mundane, routine or habitual, I want all the details of my life to reflect these values.

This does not Guarantee success or ease By any means, but there is incredible Freedom in my commitment to these core values. These Guideposts are always available no matter where I am or what I'm doing, and I don't have to spend time and energy trying to Figure out HOW to maneuver my way through any situation.

My life is not about a specific job description or title; it isn't about accomplishing a Grand Goal that the rest of the world defines as success. It is about Following my own path, expressing myself, trusting my Heart and sharing my journey. It is in all the little things that the Larger story is created, where meaning is given to every WORD, CHOICE AND INTENTION.

The story of a life is created when we Reach, Leap and TRY— sometimes succeeding, sometimes Failing, sometimes Learning our expectations Far exceeded the reality of a wished-for experience, and sometimes VICE VERSA, where unbridled joy springs up in the most surprising places.

On a snowy January day in the Midwest I visited a cemetery, and came across a grave marker peeking through the snow. All that could be seen was a portion of the word **LOVED** in gold letters, a tiny piece of evidence of what lay beneath the expansive carpet of glittering snowflakes crunching beneath my feet. As I stood among the bare trees and inhaled deeply, I contemplated all the ways our lives become uniquely empty when a loved one passes on, how we create these testaments to make sure the world understands how deeply loved those closest to us were. It is this one particular piece of a person's life that most people want remembered above all else: that they were **LOVED**.

I imaGine therl are very Few, iF any, headstones that read: SUCCESSFUL

RICH

FAMOUS

PERFECT

There are many Endeavors we can pursue in our Lives that provide a sense oF purpose and many positive attributes For which we can Be happily remembered, But Knowing the depth oF Love others Feel For us has a way oF making all the other Facets oF our Lives paLe in Comparison.

It is through the love others feel for us that our Real selves are reflected, and that is the joy we will Leave Behind* when our souls move on to new adventures.

* and also carry with us

NOW

CHOICES
18

NOW

When we focus our energy towards constructing a passionate, **MEANINGFUL** life, we are tossing a pebble into the world, creating a beautiful ripple effect of inspiration. When one person follows a dream, tries something new or takes a daring leap, everyone nearby feels that **ENERGY**, and before too long they are making their own daring leaps and inspiring yet another circle.

As this **CYCLE** continues, the world is lifted, and we are all encouraged to be that much more bold in the dreams we **CREATE** for ourselves.

tuttavia, si mostrava abbastanza commosso, perchè il Cardinale dovesse accorgersi che le sue parole non erano state senza effetto.

« Ora, » proseguì egli « l'uno fuggi-sco dalla sua casa, l'altro in procinto

Entries/Entre...

We are taught to believe we will be best served by doing things in a certain order.

1. go to school
2. get married
3. have a family
4. build a career
5. retire
6. (and then) enjoy life

But LIFE has a funny way of creating distractions, roadblocks, and other surprises, and trying to finesse our way through those hiccups can make STICKING to A PLAN rather difficult.

o tirannelli, mansuefatti, o per t

Our journey as Human Beings is not about FOLLOWING a pre-ordained path, but CREATING our own map. Life doesn't make sense because we do things "in order". Life makes sense when we stay centered in our Hearts and Learn to embrace the BEAUTIFULLY UNRULY way our journey UNFOLDS.

TIRUVANMIYUR PO <600041>
fgn-AIR-RPKT A ET411.......TN
Counter No:1,OP-Code:AI

INDIA POSTAGE
Amount:Rs122.00

22/04/2008   10:41
Wt:390grams To : USA, PIN:CA 90402

भारतीय डाक
INDIA POST

HEX929

When the term "communication barrier" is used, it tends to conjure up an image of people from different countries, none of whom can speak the other person's language. But these barriers sometimes exist no matter how well everyone understands each other's words and semantics, creating situations where spouses, siblings, and friends look at one another as if they were not just from foreign countries, but different galaxies.

45-662 EYE-EASE
45-762 20/20 BUFF
NATIONAL
Made in U.S.A.

In any conversation, exchange, or discussion, I try to imagine our communication as a game of catch. I can gently toss words and opinions to the other person so they can easily receive what I am offering, or I can hurl something forcefully without thought, kindness, or respect. I can practice deep listening and presence, or treat whoever is in front of me like an enemy.

I got hit in the face by a basketball with tremendous force in the ninth grade and I still remember the shock of the experience. Communication can feel the same way—where words sideswipe our emotions and make us feel completely thrown off guard. Our words, and the way we deliver them, have tremendous power, most especially with those we are closest to. Choices can be made every step of the way to keep the topic at hand in a space of common ground, where the intention is closeness and connection instead of being right.

Healthy communication takes effort and practice just like anything else. Flexing our "Don't take things personally" muscle is a skill requiring commitment and discipline the same way training for a marathon does. Communication barriers will always exist; the goal is not avoidance or expecting them to disappear, but learning how to move through them with our integrity and relationships intact.

29

It is easy to Fall into the trap OF wanting to GRASP - people, memories, objects, moments - but Life is not an exercise in PERMANENCE.

In our wanting, we Face a challenge that also provides the Key to our Greatest Freedom. Our LONGING to HOLD ON Gives us the opportunity to LET GO and Be content with what is in Front OF us.

Cocoons and Pupæ 43

up at the leafless trees against the sky, and if you see a queer protuberance on a branch, or a spindle-shaped swelling, or a dead leaf rolled up and clinging to a twig, get at it if you can and investigate it.

The story of a caterpillar going through a difficult, tender process in order to emerge in a more extraordinary form is a perfect metaphor for what we experience at different life stages and also when the earth feels like it is crumbling beneath us. Comparing our own process of change to something as exquisite as a butterfly enables us to focus on the beauty that can be attained within if we are willing to go through our deepest internal mines, no matter how onerous. When a caterpillar transforms into a butterfly, it is losing its familiar form in order to become something entirely different, just as periods of loss and metamorphosis alter our own interior landscapes.

Periods of significant growth and change create opportunities for us to me move away from and release habits and patterns that no longer serve us. Once we see new shapes and forms come into focus, the work of rebuilding can begin, and we start to move through the world differently.

While a caterpillar curls up into itself and does not re-surface until its entire being is transformed, we humans, with jobs, children and other responsibilities, must do our morphing in the midst of day-to-day routines. This requires effort when we might rather turn on the TV and energy when we feel on the verge of collapse. The work might not feel convenient, but without this persistence we run the risk, as Anais Nin says, "to remain tight in the bud", unable to blossom, unfurl, and FLY.

Life provides continuous cycles of transformation and growth. We become caterpillars, go into the cocoon, burst through as butterflies... and then do it all over again. The idea that we are all gorgeous winged creatures able to emerge from our darker experiences is a lovely one. and it is also important to embrace the cocoon; to cherish the times when we are deep in the act of change and shedding old selves. The in-between stages, whether delicate or turbulent, are where the most profound lessons are learned and real change occurs.

The cocoon is where we learn to slay dragons, HOWL at the moon, and embrace our flaws more compassionately ever.

The cocoon is where our souls do the work they need to do, where we are safe enough to face the truth with eyes wide open.

Let your most authentic

self be **SEEN**.

Those who annoy us teach us.
Be Grateful for the opportunities
they Give us to practice Kindness,
compassion, and Grace.

NAME
1st Notice 10/30/06
2nd Notice
Return

To create for the sake of creating

38

As an **ARTIST**, one of the experiences I love most is when someone asks what I do for a living and I get to answer, "**I AM AN ARTIST.**" Whoever asks this question usually gets a dreamy look in their eyes and is immediately intrigued, whether it is one of my husband's investment industry colleagues or a twenty-something Japanese hipster.

After the "I am an Artist" cat is out of the bag, one of the following two comments ensues, almost without fail:

`"I'm not creative at all!"`

`"I can't even draw a stick figure!"`

I find these comments humorous yet troubling. It is disheartening that so many people believe the only route to **BEING CREATIVE** is by being a **PROFESSIONAL ARTIST**, the conclusion being that if you are anything but an artist, you must not be creative.

`At all.`

39

So many people have absorbed this as an indisputable fact, and will even go so far as to argue the point with me, insisting they do not have a creative cell in their body. They believe I have been blessed by some kind of magic DNA that is given out sparingly throughout the human race.

This is astounding to me when I think about the number of colors that are now in the jumbo box of CRAYOLA CRAYONS*, how CRAYOLA has been in the coloring business since 1885 and now boasts a product line that includes markers, pencils, chalk, clay and glitter. That business would not be so thriving if there weren't hoards of children wanting to make a creative mess for one simple reason: because it's fun.

How did we get from 120 sticks of color to

"I'm not creative at all?"

40   * 120

We are all born with
a deep desire to
express ourselves.
To see the wild sense
of artistic abandonment
in children and not
recognize this
fundamental piece of
our humanity
is like trying to
stay cold in front
of a roaring fire.

they look rather formidable at first sight ;

41

Quilting. Plan mo
ly placed. Stamp c
ing. Lay waddi
th motif up. Stit
with sharp-point
adding outside stitc
ce wrong side to cove

self

42

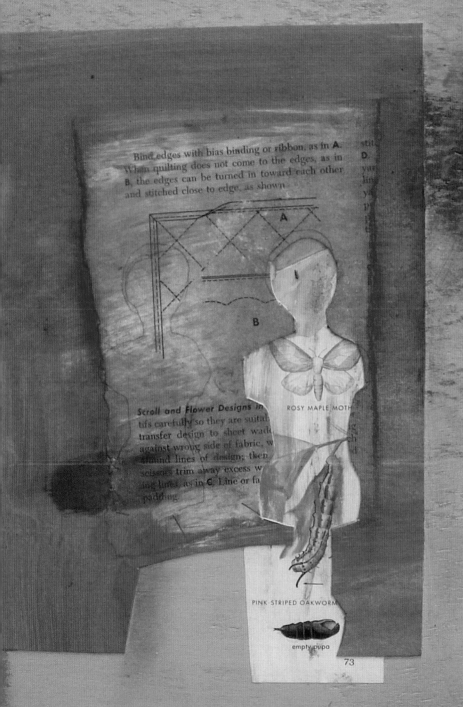

Bind edges with bias binding or ribbon, as in A. When quilting does not come to the edges, as in B, the edges can be turned in toward each other and stitched close to edge, as shown.

A

B

Scroll and Flower Designs in
tifs carefully so they are suitd
transfer design to sheet wad
against wrong side of fabric, w
found lines of design; then
scissors trim away excess w
ing lines, as in C. Line or fa
padding.

ROSY MAPLE MOTH

PINK-STRIPED OAKWORM

empty pupa

73

discovery

As I enter my fourth decade, distanced enough from the most challenging period of my life to fully appreciate all of its deeper beauty and transformative gifts, I find myself feeling the tiniest bit WISE.

Not wise in an ALL-KNOWING, I-have-it-all-figured-out kind of way, but wise in the sense that I've grown comfortably enough in my own skin to examine what this word means to me within the context of THE STORY MY LIFE IS CREATING.

Mrs Reagler Hattysburg Miss

wis·dom (wĭz′dəm) *n.* **1.** Insightful understanding of what is true, right, or enduring. **2.** Native good judgment <had the *wisdom* to leave well enough alone> **3.** The amassed learning of philosophers, scientists, and scholars.
wisdom tooth *n.* The last tooth on each side of both jaws in humans.
wise¹ (wīz) *adj.* **wis·er, wis·est. 1.** Having great learning. **2.** Having discernment **:** sagacious. **3.** Sensible **:** prudent. **4. a.** Having awareness or information **:** knowing. **b.** Cunning **:** shrewd. **5.** *Slang.* Offensively bold or impudent. **—wise′ly** *adv.*
wise² (wīz) *n.* Manner or fashion <in this *wise*>
-wise *suff.* **1.** In a given way, direction, or position <counterclock*wise*> **2.** *Informal.* Regarding <dollar*wise*>
wise·a·cre (wīz′ā′kər) *n. Informal.* One who pretends to be learned or clever.
wise·crack (wīz′krăk′) *n. Slang.* A witty or facetious remark. **—wise′crack′** *v.*
wish (wĭsh) *n.* **1.** A desire or longing for something. **2.** An expression of a wish <Make a *wish*.> **3.** Something desired. **—v. 1.** To desire or long for **:** want. **2.** To make or express a wish for <*wished* us a safe trip> **3.** To bid <*wish* someone good night> **4.** To request or command <I *wish* you to go at once.> **5.** To force or impose upon another. **—wish′er** *n.*

I believe wisdom is having an awareness of all the questions we can explore in any given situation.

I believe it is becoming more at ease with not having absolute answers.

I believe it is about choosing to live with integrity even when no one is watching about living by my highest standards regardless of the choices those around me make.

I believe wisdom is about accepting life's difficulties and recognizing all the beauty available to me on this very bumpy journey.

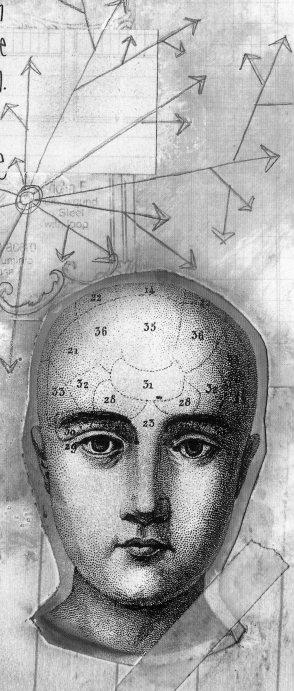

I Believe it is about Being GENTLE
with MYSELF and those around me,
about reCoGnizinG all the tender
places we share as Human BeinGs
wHo are all SEARCHING For meaninG,
comFort, love, SHelter and may Be
even the PERFECT SUNSET.

47

It is about Getting Lost in the Journey of my Questions rather than insisting on always BEING RIGHT.

It is about draining the tension out of my Heart, mind and BODY during periods of uncertainty and appreciating that such experiences are more about WIDE OPEN POSSIBILITY than impending DOOM.

The more I ACCEPT that my most profound Questions are ultimately unknowable and the less emphasis I place on perfection, certainty, and security, the wiser I Feel.

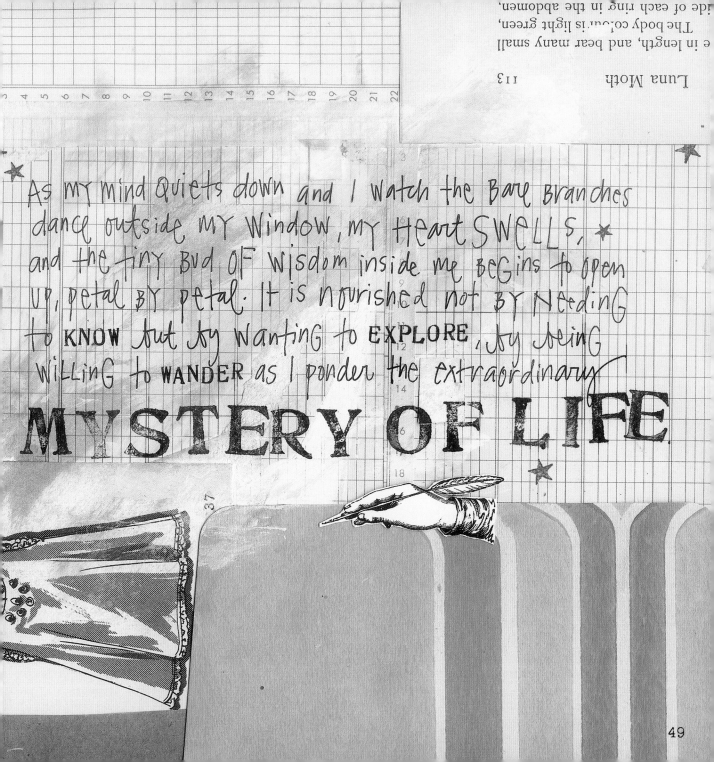

As my mind quiets down and I watch the bare branches dance outside my window, my heart swells, and the tiny bud of wisdom inside me begins to open up, petal by petal. It is nourished not by needing to **KNOW** but by wanting to **EXPLORE**, by being willing to **WANDER** as I ponder the extraordinary

MYSTERY OF LIFE

REFUGE building
HOME
dwelling
residence house retreat
NEST
Shelter COTTAGE
haven

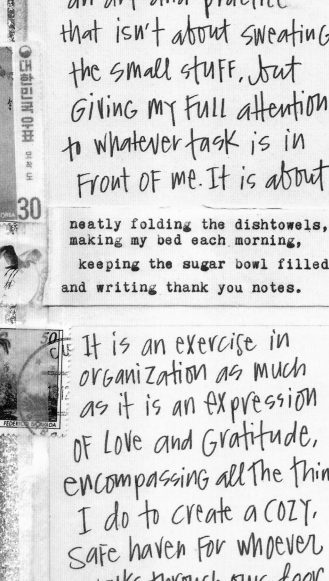

Mother Teresa implores us to

"do small things with great love,"

an art and practice that isn't about sweating the small stuff, but giving my full attention to whatever task is in front of me. It is about

neatly folding the dishtowels, making my bed each morning, keeping the sugar bowl filled, and writing thank you notes.

It is an exercise in organization as much as it is an expression of love and gratitude, encompassing all the things I do to create a cozy, safe haven for whoever walks through our door.

50

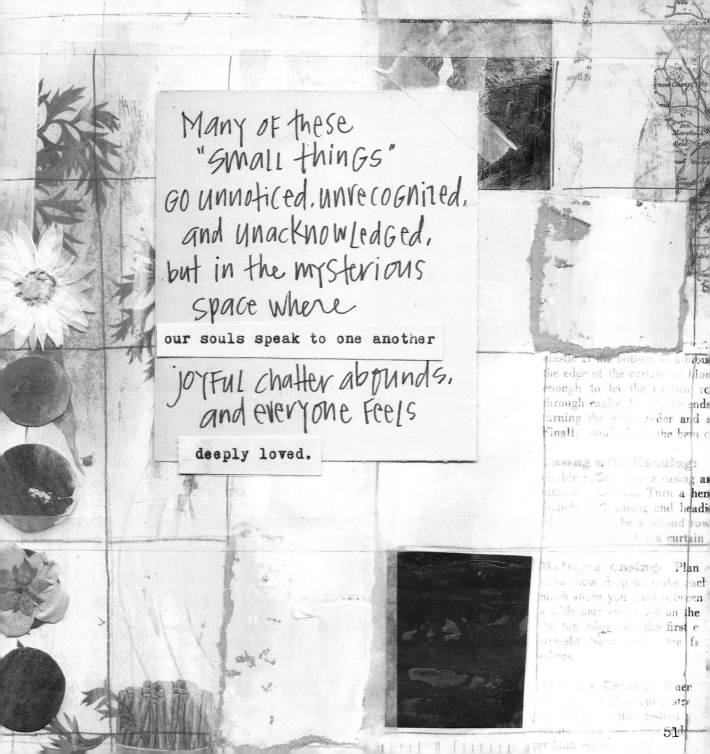

Many of these "small things" Go unnoticed, unrecognized, and unacknowledged, but in the mysterious space where

our souls speak to one another

joyful chatter abounds, and everyone feels

deeply loved.

Family is a complicated word. It comes up—in a conversation, a movie, or maybe a book—and I have to immediately tame the whirlwind of ideas, images, desires, fears, and dreams it inspires. It challenges me in a myriad of moments to take a deep breath, stay present, and send away the gremlins it loves to stir up.

I lived in a frustrating state of confusion about the subject for most of my life, trying to figure out what family meant to me. I had all kinds of examples of how other people defined and created family, but no clear direction for myself.

Finding my way towards the path - and family - where I belonged was a creative act like anything else. Even now, when I am able to embrace the idea of family more fully than ever, I must choose to be fully engaged with this practice day in and day out. Creating, nurturing and *strengthening* my family is an ongoing journey. I want my actions to reflect my intention, and my intention is to keep my family *intact*.

18
19
20
21
22
23
24
25
26
27
28
29
30
31
32
33
34
35
36
37
38
39
40

In a world full of so much uncertainty, family is something we want to be able to rely on no matter what. Despite this deep human yearning, it is rare to meet someone who has a completely stable family with no baggage, anger, or deep regret. Families are complex entities made up of Human Beings, everyone trying to make their way in the world. All those dreams, memories, and experiences rubbing up against each other sometimes create conflict; however strong the current of love and loyalty is between family members, notions of what family means, requires, and can endure will likely be challenged.

16
17

Whatever we might have been taught to believe about family - at any point in our lives - will someday be called into question. Whatever we thought we knew or believed was true, we will end up developing our own definition and sense of family whether we set out to or not. This can be a profound turning point - when we shed the ideals of our parents or society or maybe even The Brady Bunch and construct our own. They might not end up looking or feeling *wildly* different from what we've been taught, but the act of making them uniquely ours is an opportunity for empowerment, independence and individuation.

I understand family not as a static, permanent entity. but a tribe of people I Love, have a history with, and am related to. that contracts and expands in different circumstances. I don't know if my definition of family is "normal" or "correct", I only know it is MINE, and how hard I worked to create it.

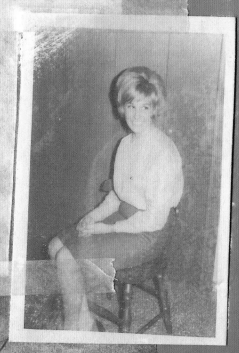

28 29 30 31 32 33 34 35 36 37 38

MONTGOMERY,
CORSICANA, TEXAS

Merle
Evelyne
Robert
Doris
Dorothy
Geneva
Christine
Waleta
Joseph
Mattie
Harry
Sadie
John
Maggie
Opal
Jewel
Rose
Frank
Bessie
Nell
Ernestine
Alvin
Patricia
Ruth
Walter
Lois
Suzanne

Grand moments are nice, but it is the smaller gems that create the most exquisite beauty, the tiny jewels that adorn our lives every single day.

57

All I was doing was washing dishes, on an evening like every other evening that week where my husband and I met each other at our kitchen table later than usual for dinner, both exhausted from running around like lunatics all day. It being December, he was dealing with a huge end of the year to do list at work and I was playing my annual role as Santa Claus, in charge of all things Christmas. We had a simple meal, and I was cleaning up as he sat at his laptop hunting for gifts when I looked over at him and suddenly felt a gentle wave of contentment melt into me like a drop of honey in hot tea. It was as if there was a force in the world that wanted to make sure I recognized how precious that moment was, and in that strangely poetic instance, I saw it with perfect clarity: **this is it**.

This is the life we have worked so hard to create.

These are the moments we Get to enjoy...Quiet nights at home when we share our days with each other, eat a home-cooked meal, read a book and later, fall asleep next to each other in a cozy bed and perfect silence.

this is our consummate joy.

As much as life's extraordinary moments are powerful in their own way, I often find the quieter ones more meaningful, more lovely in their simplicity. I am the only person in the world who Gets to create and share a home with my husband, with all the tiny details that entails. It is within those specifics that the simple becomes the divine, the "normal" becomes wholly unique.

That evening—for no reason in particular—was its own tiny universe, an instant that encompassed every other instant of my wonderfully imperfect life... and I held it like a fragile, dainty butterfly that wanted nothing more than for me to stop and notice it.

Then in one quick instant,
it fluttered away.

and Before I could Blink,

it was Gone.

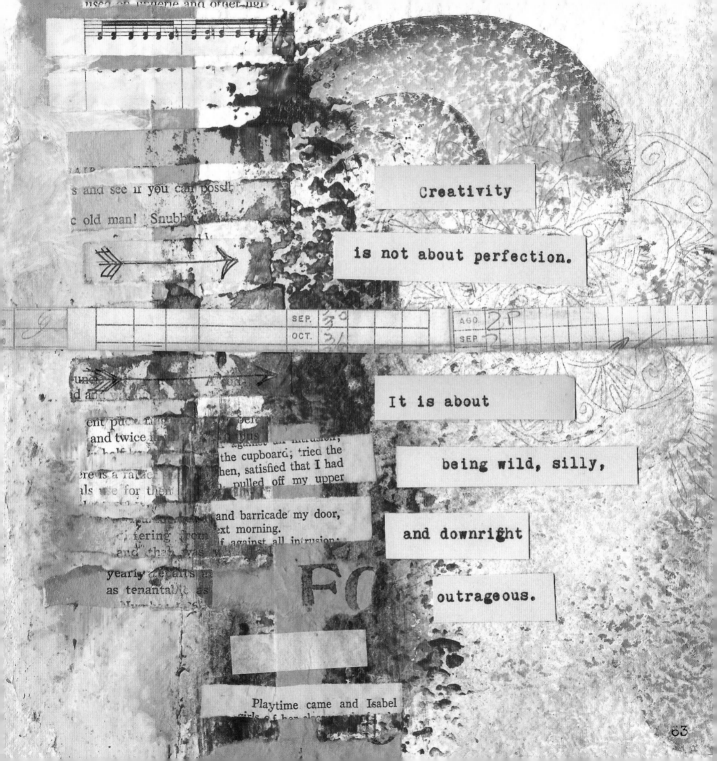

Creativity

is not about perfection.

It is about

being wild, silly,

and downright

outrageous.

"HOW DID YOU LEARN HOW TO DO IT?"

...is the question I usually get in any discussion about my greeting card business, and my answer is always the same: by doing everything wrong the first time.

From figuring out how to create a purchase order form to arranging images for my printer, that was my modus operandi, and while I did not set out to learn everything I needed to know by making mistakes, I must admit it was a very effective learning tool.

½ 1 2 3 4 5 6 7 8 9 10 11 12 13 14

After four decades of amassing heaps of mistakes professionally and otherwise, I have developed a very specific philosophy about them, the key point being that mistakes do not equal failure.

Mistakes are simply human.

They can result when trying something new, taking steps towards a dream, interacting with our friends as well as when cooking, driving and even spelling. Mistakes are part of life, and without them our journey would be a lot less interesting.

Even when we do our best, it is possible we will *make mistakes*. Knowing this, we can choose to live in fear of them or accept that they just might happen and, when they do, take responsibility. Trying to run away from our errors and missteps only serves to increase the time we spend dealing with them; the choice to stand up and say, "I made a mistake," immediately frees us from unnecessary baggage. We might have to take time to correct our blunders and make amends, but it will create forward movement and positive action. Attempts made to cover up, shift blame, or avoid responsibility have a way of pulling us down in the muck, unable to move beyond whatever didn't go as planned.

In doing just about everything incorrectly the first time I tried anything as I built Swirly, I felt very clumsy and inept. Looking back, it is easy to see that my mistakes were the result of inexperience more than anything else. Beyond those details, it was the journey of many tiny missteps that helped me learn how to maneuver my way through all the fumbles I continue to make from a place of confidence, grace, and integrity. I learned over and over again that my mistakes did not take away from the truth that I was smart, capable, creative, or doing my best — they only meant that I wasn't infallible.

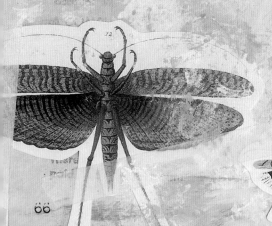

edge of straight table as measurer.

Using an automatic skirt marker.

In all of our unique slips and stumbles,
we learn about ourselves and We Grow.

We Find the way to hold our head high
in' our imperfections and have confidence in
ourselves through our blunders.

We discover it is possible to SOAR
even if we've tripped, bumped, teetered, or tottered,
that sometimes losing our footing enables
us to take Greater Leaps than we
thought possible.

I believe it is possible for every element of my life to interconnect in a way that makes it feel less like a pressure-filled balancing act and more like an extraordinary, creative

EXPERIMENT

where every act, no matter how mundane, is a piece of the puzzle that creates my very best life

SAFETY MATCHES

2⁰ PISO

70

We all have people in our lives who we want to impress, who we hope will like us, who we want to make proud. In any relationship, the important thing to remember is that this kind of respect should not be given away haphazardly. Your deepest devotion should be granted to those who like you, are impressed by you, and proud of you BECAUSE YOU'RE YOU.

You will Find your way to Like·minded Souls BY **BEING YOURSELF** and creating a Life according to your Values. The more you try to Squeeze Yourself into Someone else's Mold, the more contentment will drain From your Spirit.

* * * * * * *

I tried desperately to Squeeze myself into a teeny tiny Box For Someone else For a very Long time. This Box represented the amount of room this person had in his Heart For an authentic relationship with me. He was interested in a relationship with me **IF AND ONLY IF** our interactions were exclusively on his terms and according to his ideas OF who I ought to Be and How I ought to Behave.

I ALLOWED THIS FOR MANY YEARS.

Then one day I had no choice but to break out of the box, and the instant I did this he became unbearably cruel, accusing me of being all the things I strive NOT to be - selfish, ungrateful, foolish, without integrity.

It took a while, but I finally realized the absolute truth of this situation — that whatever this person's opinion of me, it need not have ANY impact on me because this person DID NOT KNOW ME AT ALL.

Our "relationship" had been built around the fact that I existed in the TINY BOX, so whatever he (thought) he knew about me, or chose to believe about me, was based on interactions in which I never authentically shared myself. I shared only as much as what could fit in the box, and the rest I kept hidden.

What he experienced was a shadow of me, self-perpetuated by my desire to earn his love. I literally blocked my own sunlight, and this seemed to please him. I gave him this power for a LONG time.

Once I unchained myself from this relationship, all the control I had offered him unquestioningly returned to me, and I learned how to soar like never before. As painful as facing the truth of our dynamic was, it gave me the strength to stand firm in my own integrity and rooted in my own self.

****

Letting go of these relationships, as healthy as this might be in the long run, can still cause a unique kind of grief, but in the destruction and dismantling, new space opens up for your most authentic self to emerge. You deserve to move through this world committed to your own ideals and strongest sense of self, and there are people the world over who want nothing more from you than to see your wings spread wide, glimmering across a

PERFECT BLUE SKY.

"Life has taught me that it is filled with unbelievable beauty, limitless opportunities and untold miracles.

"One must take the time to understand it, to appreciate it and to live it. Just think, all of a sudden, when you wake up each morning, life isn't life — IT'S LIFE! It is beyond belief."

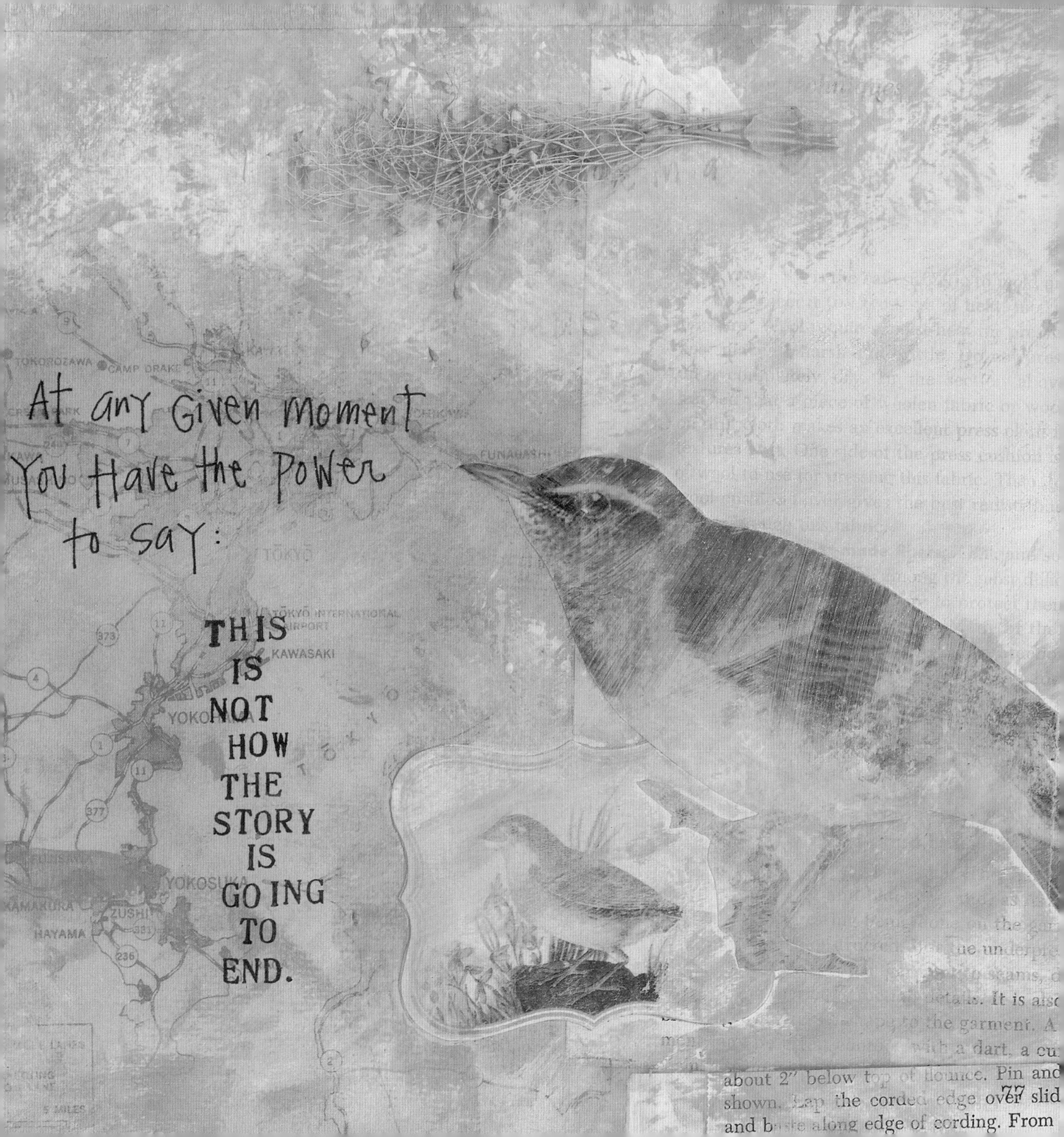

At any Given moment
You Have the Power
to say:

THIS
IS
NOT
HOW
THE
STORY
IS
GOING
TO
END.

FULLY

LiViNG a LiFe ↓ Committed to one's
strongest Values is not a way OF
LiFe for the meek, the FeARFuL,
or the SQueamish. It is a Way OF
LiFe that I Sometimes Curse myseLF
For choosinG, especially in
those moments when the
ALLure OF WALLoWING and GiViNG
up Shines BRIGHTLY in my
peripheral Vision, wanting to
puLL me in Like a moth to a
Flame. Those are the moments
when I want to be LAzy and take
whatever is the easiest way out...
and run the Greatest risk OF
Losing my way.

Those are the crucial moments when I must dig deep and stay focused on being the kind of person I strive to be.

It is easy to practice compassion with those who are kind to me, more challenging with those who are hurtful.

It is in those moments when the standards I set → **for myself** ← are truly tested, and if I am able to walk through them with my integrity intact, I have succeeded in the most profound way I am capable of succeeding as a Human Being in a complicated world.

DREAM

BELIEVE

GROW

WANDER

HOPE

FLY

SANBON KAKI / GOHON KAKI

三本花器/五本花器

庭で摘んだお花を一
どんなふうに飾る
考えながら花を
大切にしたい時

You pick up the flower

farther

TO BE LOVED... to travel
through the world and create
a life beneath a halo
of beloved-ness, beneath the
light created by the act
of someone making a choice
to love ya... this is our

Greatest journey.

we have to be willing to let
others into our peculiar little
worlds to bask under this
exquisite, penetrating light.

In any relationship, many problems—maybe even ALL—are not based on anything REAL, but are instead created and nurtured by a laundry list of fears. Fears we carry with us and fears that others in our vicinity throw into the mix. It is as if we all agree to believe the myth that we exist in dark rooms apart from one another, but the truth is that we are TOGETHER in a wide open field where we can all have what we desire, and the desires we each LONG for are the same:

※ We want to be close.

※ We want to feel safe.

❋ We want to be connected.

※ And we are afraid.

we will very likely always have to wrestle with our unique mixed bag of fears. From time to time they may interrupt the otherwise pleasant back and forth volley of dreams, thoughts & emotions we have with those we love and care about.

As much as it is possible, we need to have compassion for those fears rather than disdain, to recognize that they are soft spots in our hearts rather than walls around them. They are spaces that have

TREMENDOUS CAPACITY FOR GROWTH.

Because if we can help one another move beyond these fears and replace them with greater levels of trust, we can move to a truly sacred existence where love is the Guiding Force.

[For Taylor]

Or are you looking for...
...in California?

SERVICE STATION AND GARAGE
No. 426 – $3600. You can...
your own for just $3600...
...station selling item...

very curious

84

every single moment you are writing the story of your life.

In an age when the phenomenal success and generosity of Oprah Winfrey stands as the shining example of what it means to BE **inspiring**, it is easy to fall into the trap of thinking our choices and actions won't make a difference, let alone be counted as "inspirational." But inspiration exists everywhere, in **everything** we do from the moment we wake up to the instant we fall asleep. In the midst of meals, errands, work, and play, what we do has an impact on Humanity.

We are all making our way through a complicated society that is filled with distractions, frustrations, and injustice. We are all on a quest for meaning, trekking through our own internal jungles to find the answers we seek. As we weave the tapestry of our own lives, we are each capable of acting as a beacon-as inspirational beings who others look to for guidance, joy and,wisdom.

We each inspire, delight,
and contribute to the world
by creating a cozy home,
showing kindness to a stranger.
Writing a poem, laughing out loud.
Saying No, saying Yes,
    saying I'm sorry, saying i love you.

All of these Gestures and countless others
emit a **radiant light**, and the
world needs as much light as possible...

Light from every smile,
    every gentle word,
every daring leap.

給　料
(給料明細書在中)

No.

月分

所属

殿

ready to transform,

When you are standing at the bottom of a Mountain that you have no choice but to climb, taking one day at a time is the only thing that matters. It is the only way you will reach the top of that Mountain, the

only way you will find your way through the darkness.

IT IS SOLID.

It is reliable. It is like the rising of the sun everyday— it is something you might not take much time to notice, but it is always there, a reminder that each new day holds endless possibility.

LEGS

FEET

I travel to learn about the world, to smell the aromas of a strange city, and drink the colors of a foreign land. I travel to meet friends that are now living their lives on another part of the planet, totally unaware of the fact that we will someday find our way to each other.

I travel for all of these reasons and more, but beyond all the joy I experience when I embark to a new spot on the world atlas, I travel to discover myself, as that terrain is sometimes the strangest and most unfamiliar of all...

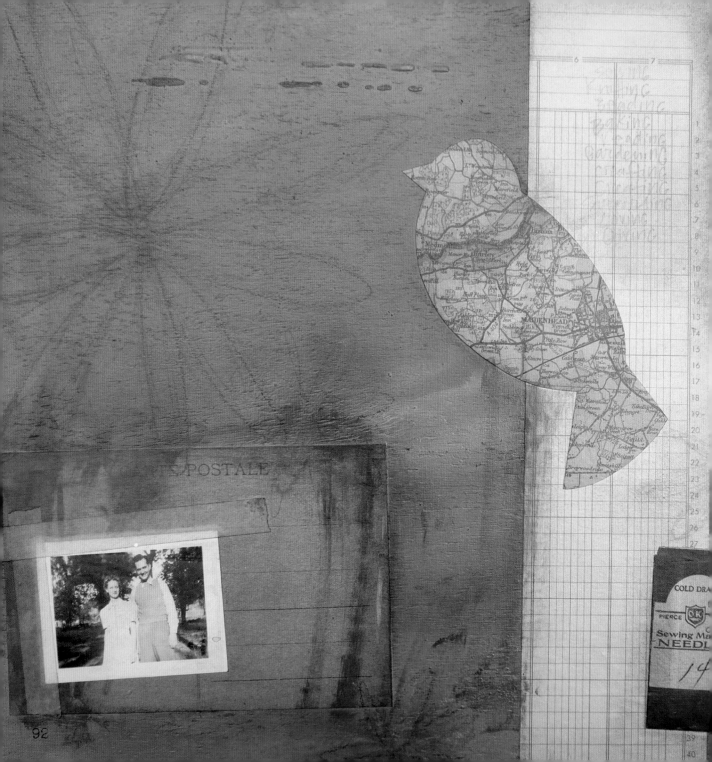

OH how I have **failed!**
In relationships, in Business, in Freshman Chemistry at Virginia Tech. In a multitude of places, **i have failed.**

And I have failed for one simple reason: Because I've **tried.**

In any effort, failure is a possibility.
And Beyond any failure, there is always room to **try again.**

SIERRA DE LOS ORGANOS

93

I do not Wish For an **EASY LIFE.*** I do not WALK this earth imaGininG how much Better my life Could Be iF only **THIS** or iF only **THAT**. I have dreams I want to pursue, Goals I want to accomplish, and experiences I want to enjoy, but Beyond any WantinG, imaGininG, and hopinG, I also nurture a Quiet space in my LiFe For **ACCEPTANCE**. A space where I can Lean deeper into whatever miGht Feel less than ideal and explore whether or not my initial judGments were accurate. OFten times what I thouGht miGht Be a Source oF unendinG woe turns out to Be an

incredible blessing.

*** This feels rather silly to say because compared to most I have an incredibly easy life.**

How often do we spend time and energy searching for, trying to find, or hoping to construct some image of "PERFECT," some definition we have decided is the only way we can possibly find contentment?

How many gifts and treasures are overlooked because our attention is so fiercely focused on what is not available?

When I wake up each day, I do not set out to create an existence of "perfect." I instead try to open myself up as much as possible to all the perfect moments that exist in an imperfect life.

96

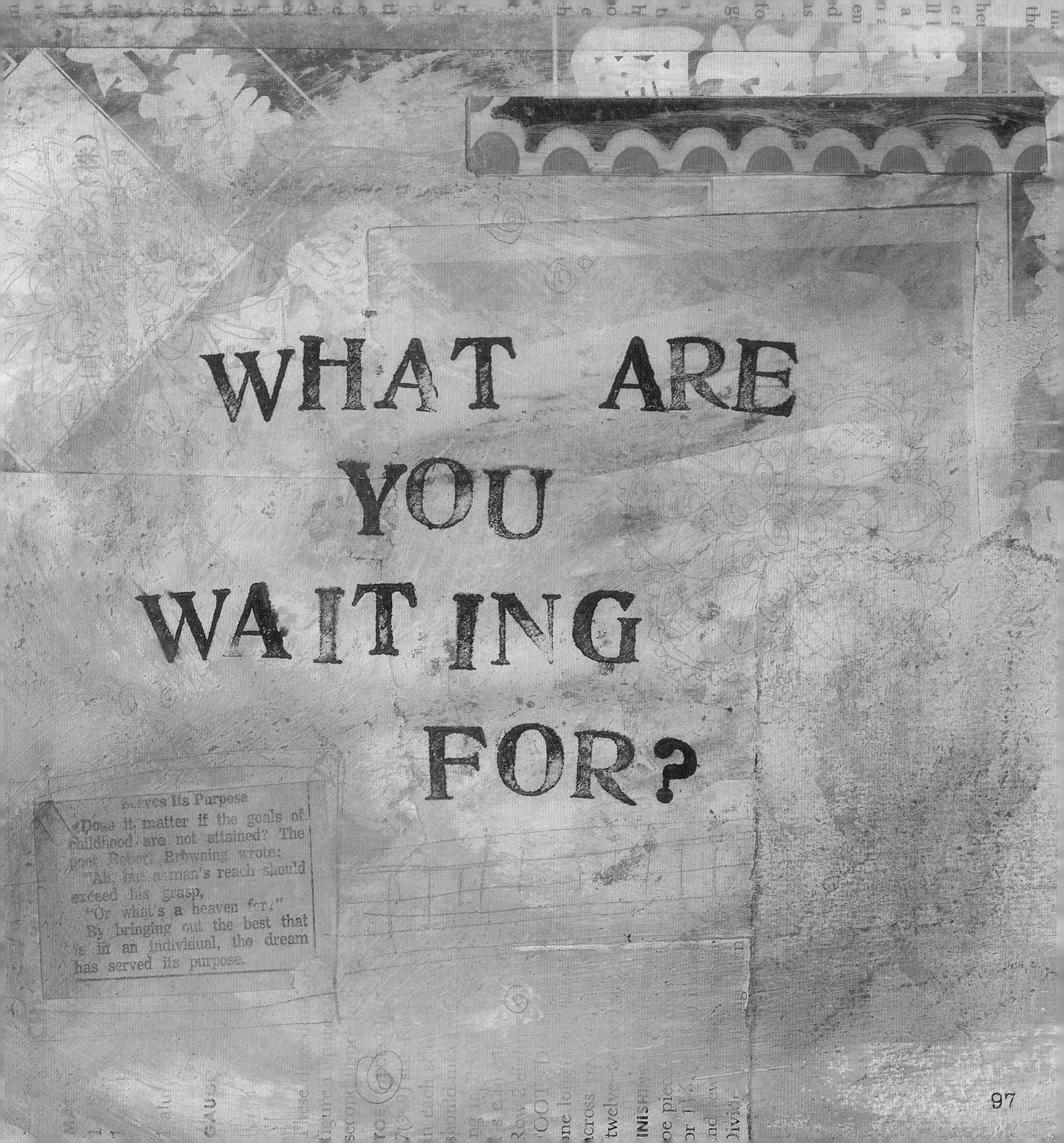

WHAT ARE YOU WAITING FOR?

Serves Its Purpose

Does it matter if the goals of childhood are not attained? The poet Robert Browning wrote:

"Ah, but a man's reach should exceed his grasp,

"Or what's a heaven for."

By bringing out the best that is in an individual, the dream has served its purpose.

Soon after my husband and I got settled into our new home in Los Angeles, we had friends over for dinner who gave us a bottle of Dom Perignon champagne as a housewarming gift. This was a very special treat, and we immediately put the bottle in our refrigerator, deciding we would save it for a *special occasion.*

MAY	JUNE	JULY	AUGUST	SEPTEMBER	OCTOBER	NOVEMBER	DEC
M T W T F S	S M T W T F S	S M T W T F S	S M T W T F S	S M T W T F S	S M T W T F S	S M T W T F S	S M T
. . 1 2 3 4 5	. . . . . . 1 2	1 2 3 4 5 6 7	. . . . 1 2 3 4	 1	. . 1 2 3 4 5 6	. . . . . 1 2 3	. . 1
. 7 8 9 10 11 12	3 4 5 6 7 8 9	8 9 10 11 12 13 14	5 6 7 8 9 10 11	2 3 4 5 6 7 8	7 8 9 10 11 12 13	4 5 6 7 8 9 10	2 3 9 10 11
14 15 16 17 18 19	10 11 12 13 14 15 16	15 16 17 18 19 20 21	12 13 14 15 16 17 18	9 10 11 12 13 14 15	14 15 16 17 18 19 20	11 12 13 14 15 16 17	16 17 18
21 22 23 24 25 26	17 18 19 20 21 22 23	22 23 24 25 26 27 28	19 20 21 22 23 24 25	16 17 18 19 20 21 22	21 22 23 24 25 26 27	18 19 20 21 22 23 24	23 24 25
28 29 30 31 . . .	24 25 26 27 28 29 30	29 30 31	26 27 28 29 30 31 .	23 24 25 26 27 28 29	28 29 30 31 . . .	25 26 27 28 29 30 . .	30 31
				30			

Many months later, with the bottle still waiting for that "perfect moment" to be uncorked, we decided to cook a simple dinner at home. Out of the blue, my husband brought out the bottle, deciding that would be the night we enjoyed it. Our special occasion turned out to be nothing more than a quiet Sunday evening with a cozy dinner for two in our living room.

We opened the champagne, it was delightful, and have since considered that evening a special occasion for no reason other than we decided to make it one. We could have waited for some other evening with greater significance and used that as an excuse to open the champagne, but instead we popped the cork on what looked like an average evening and transformed it into something extraordinary.

There are so many circumstances, situations, and dreams that make us believe we have to wait for the PERFECT TIME. Whether buying a house, having children, starting a business, or trying a new hobby we decide, too often, everything will be easier if we wait... and wait... until all areas of our lives are in perfect alignment.

With this determination, it is all too easy to fall into a pattern of exploring our dreams and tucking them away for *Later*.

"When I have a bigger studio."

"When I have more money."

"When all my laundry is done."

whatever our visions or dreams, they hold

mystery, uncertainty, adventure, and wonder,

all of which propel us forward the instant we say,

 "NOW is the time."

Before too long, we will come to understand the unique perfection of that moment - of all the ways it clicked everything into place exactly when it needed to. It isn't possible for us to understand all the intricacies of our dreams ahead of time; in releasing the idea that our best-laid plans will be foolproof and unfold exactly the way we've outlined, we open ourselves up to even greater possibilities than we'd imagined. We create magic where it might have looked drab, we invite the miraculous into an otherwise "normal" day.

We can plan and scheme and plot,

or we can simply choose to BEGIN,

Butterick PRINTED PATTERN

HIP

BLOUSE PATTERN
NOT INCLUDED

収入
新

A

Your wings already exist.
All you have to do is

FLY

The world wants
to see them.

A

〒100-6335 東京都千代田区丸の内2-4-1
電話 03 (5220) 3170 FAX 03 (3240) 1031
丸の内ビルディング35F

お歳暮 天婦羅

領収証

No.

17年 7月 16日

QUICK
AND
EASY

My First Visit to Tokyo was not about seeing specific landmarks and marking them off a tour guide checklist. It was about observing a new city with its own unique traits, quirks, and norms that are far different from my own in the United States. It was about leaving my hotel room and entering an entirely different environment and not wanting to stick out like an obnoxious, disrespectful sore thumb. Each situation I encountered — a meal, shopping, navigating the subway system, taking a taxi — gave me an opportunity to be still, observe, and follow what the locals did. Each day was an exercise in releasing assumptions that my way of doing things was best, or even appropriate, and opening myself up to something I had not yet considered or experienced.

In Tokyo, there is a particular way you give a salesperson your credit card (with both hands, placing it on a small tray). There is a particular way whatever you buy is packaged (very neatly, very securely- even a washcloth). There is a specific way boxes are wrapped, a pattern of haphazard-looking folds where only one piece of tape is needed to hold it all together.

All of these details I noticed and learned by allowing myself the time to absorb my surroundings slowly rather than plowing through the day trying to cram in as many activities and sights as possible.

I went to Tokyo thinking I would feel lost, disconnected, and disoriented. Instead, I felt oddly at home. I appreciated the gracefulness of the people, the attention to detail, and the peculiar way the city felt quiet despite all the cars and people. Most everyone was quite reserved, but I found myself practically stalking a group of teenage girls one afternoon, giggling at how clearly I saw my own my own teenage self in them — full of high pitched squeals of nervous laughter, with Hello Kitty paraphernalia dangling from purses, necklaces, and keychains, clinking and jingling everywhere they went. I imagined them in school, staring at the boys they thought were the cutest, and gathering together like this each day to swoon and dream over milkshakes and metallic pink cell phones. Are we, as human beings, really so different from each other? Sometimes yes, many times, not so much.

YUZEN

ORIGAMI
105

I realize I only saw one small layer of life in Tokyo, and as a 5'7" blonde, I was viewed and treated by everyone I came into contact with as an obvious foreigner. This was not bad, but different from how they interact with friends & family; I don't believe I gained any special insight into Japanese life or Tokyo's social norms. As is true of all my travel experiences, what I learned most about was myself - my ability to adapt, my cultural biases, my fears, and all the other things I carry with me as I wander on my own in a new city that speaks a strange language. As I walked in unfamiliar neighborhoods and watched an old woman ride her bike through a cemetary with a basket of flowers, I was alone with my thoughts.

It is always in this particular kind of alone-ness I make startling discoveries - about the world and my self.

I do not travel to follow itineraries.

BONte002 アンケートご回答

I travel to see whatever I happen to see.

I travel to challenge myself, to step outside of myself, and hopefully return home slightly changed, maybe even slightly wiser.

All it takes is a willingness to wander, to make mistakes, to ask for help, to observe, to follow my instincts,

to face fears, and step outside my comfort zone.

This is true when I travel to a new place and in so many

other situations — when I begin a work of art, when I argue with my husband.

It is true no matter what...
every single day,
wherever I happen to be.

13   ペンネーム (   )   希望プレゼント番号   1 ・ 2 ・ 3

107

Life can be adorned with many wonderful experiences, accomplishments and even **MATERIAL OBJECTS**, but the deepest joy exists in those rare instances of **CLARITY**, when there is no wanting, no yearning, no clinging to any idealized life we believe exists somewhere other than **EXACTLY** where we are.

RAT DE POCHE

EXTRA BUTTONS

110

Many years ago, in the midst of one of the most challenging episodes of my life, a dear friend said seven small words to me:

"ALL YOU HAVE TO DO IS RECEIVE."

The very instant those words were punctuated with a tiny period, they became embedded in my psyche, and I have since carried them with me everywhere I go, passing them out like daisies in quiet conversations over coffee and broken hearts.

Whenever I share those words with someone, regardless of the circumstances, the reaction to this truth is curiously consistent: there is an almost imperceptible pause, followed by a nod that is slightly reticent and painfully tender. It is a moment when I am able to observe the unveiling of another person's vulnerability, when seven little words act as links in a chain that pull even the toughest defenses down, if only for a moment.

To receive is something many seem to struggle with, very often over concerns that someone else's giving will deplete them of some all-important item:

* time
* energy
* money
* Love

Being told it is OK to receive freely and without guilt touches the most delicate place in our hearts. For when we are given permission to Receive, we are being told something else as well, something even more important: that we are worthy and deserving of all the Love and support we need.

There are times in Life when we are called upon to Give, and times when the world needs us to Receive. We must offer ourselves in both arenas, knowing they each feed and inspire the world. We Give. We take. We Ask, we Receive, and in all of these exchanges, we contribute.

114

We would all prefer to experience as little emotional pain and Heartache as possible, but must be discerning in our Quest to steer Clear of any potential despair. If not Kept at Bay, Fear can Quietly Close our Hearts to the extraordinary Bliss that Can Be Had if we are willing to Love

WITH ABANDON.

The more we aspire to avoid pain, the more we lose sight of all the joy

SURRENDER

Has to Offer... surrender to Love, to Beauty, and the wild unknown of Both.

117

Being an ARTiST is something I have Been doing From the time I could WALK, and what I always dreamed For MYSELF Growing up. I consider it a tremendous Honor to Be aBle to say "I am an artist", and I still say it with a slightly stunned tingling in my Heart. Part OF me doesn't Feel Like it is REAL, and another part OF me sometimes doesn't Feel Like I deserve it.

But it is WHO I AM and WHAT I DO and I have Learned to Create my own DeFinition OF what it means to BE AN ARTIST.

It is tempting to insert the word "SUCCESSFUL" BeFore "Artist" in that sentence, But these two words Feel redundant when reFerring to my own LiFe. I AM AN ARTiST, and Being aBle to say this is my Greatest achievement.

It is just that simple.

So there you have it: my greatest success story in four words

I have enjoyed a variety of accomplishments as an ARtist through assorted media, creations, ideas, projects, and ventures, but through everything it is that one tiny piece of my life that fills me with the deepest contentment.

I am an artist.

I say this and smile, and in those first few seconds when the words are still lingering in the air, my Heart Glows a Little Bit Brighter and joy radiates from every cell in my Body.

I am an artist.

This is the Greatest treasure; this is the most precious Gift.

This is my Success.

LOVELIEST OF TREES

A. E. Housman

Loveliest of trees, the cherry now
Is hung with bloom along the bough,
And stands about the woodland ride
Wearing white for Eastertide.

Now, of my threescore years and ten,
Twenty will not come again,
And take from seventy springs a score,
It only leaves me fifty more.

And since to look at things in bloom
Fifty springs are little room,
About the woodlands I will go
To see the cherry hung

In my experiences as a woman who follows her dreams as much as possible, I have been blessed with many dreams come true. I have also had my share of flops and a few dreams made real that reminded me to

be careful about what I wish for.

Through all of this, I have come to believe that there is one element above all others that will have the greatest impact on my ability to not only make a dream real but to also enjoy it every step of the way:

CERTIFIED MAIL™

expectations.

It is fascinating to explore my past and see all the threads of experience that led me to right now, to see how much it all makes sense... that the foundation of my personality was formed at an incredibly young age and hasn't changed much since then. I have traveled, learned and experienced much, but the essence of who I am and how I live my life is inextricably linked to who I was when I was still running around my house in a costume pretending to be Wonder Woman.

The labels I consisently attach
to myself — Artist
            Wanderer
                Philosopher —

all have their origins in the journey
I started years ago when I would
chase fireflies on warm summer
nights and quench my thirst with a
garden hose, when I needed nothing
more than an empty refrigerator
box and a few crayons to create
my own magic castle.

I'm still that girl.

And she's just fine, exactly
    the way she is.

ABBREVIATIONS

sts)

. . . . stitch (es)

— this symbol indicates tha[t]
diately following are to be r[epeated]
ber of times.

STITCH GAUGE: A
to a specified stitch
size needles with wh[ich]
tain the stitch gauge
However, if you do no[t]
the suggested needle
will give you the spe[cified]
at the stitch gauge gi[ven]
work to be the size gi[ven]

MATERIALS REQUIRE[D]

1 BERNAT Gold L[abel]
1 pair plastic knit[ting]
or women's size
1 pair plastic k[nitting]

[G]AUGE 7 sts

Teach me your mood, O patient stars!
Who climb each night the ancient sky,
Leaving on space no shade, no scars,
No trace of age, no fear to die.

—R. W. Emers[on]

how uncomfortable it is
my fears, anxieties
comfort zones and beliefs
about the world are
being shattered and
reconfigured. Being in
Havana is thrilling,
unnerving, shocking
and oh so beautiful.

Havana 2010

Sometimes we must be willing to let go
of that one thing we think defines us,
that part of ourselves we believe makes us
who we are;
the idea of taking a torch to definitions
we have assigned to ourselves can be
frightening, but after the destruction,
after the raging fires that may ensue,
new growth will always —always—
spring forth, in places we might
have believed were incapable of
sustaining life.

日本法令 注文番号 給与9-3

when things fall apart, it is time to **rebuild**, and in this moment we have the choice to try to re-create what we had before or start fresh with new materials. In late 2001, when I was in the midst of trying to pick up and re-assemble all the pieces of my life, I was faced with such a choice. After wandering around aimlessly trying to figure out my next steps, I had an epiphany in the oddest of places — in my car on an unremarkable day, at a stop sign in front of the Santa Barbara Mission. For some inexplicable reason — call it a flash of insight or a message from the heavens — a thought came flooding into my brain: it was time to be a GROWN UP. It was time to let go of old ways of being and forge an entirely new path. In that instant, I took my first step.

Until that realization hit me over the head like a coconut, I had been playing the ROLE of a GROWN UP without really embracing it as a key piece of my identity. I had been doing Grown Up things without taking the accompanying responsibilities to heart, trying to be "wise", "sophisticated", and "mature" without understanding that those traits are authentic only when they are embedded in something more fundamental, which is a conscious commitment to being a Grown Up.

Becoming a Grown Up was a decision I made after realizing I had not been doing my best. When so much was lost and I felt unmoored from just about everything I had built my life around, I was compelled to take stock in the choices I had made and the priorities that had been guiding me. This did not mean my heart had to die, that life was no longer fun, or that I couldn't still be wacky and impulsive at times. It meant I took responsibility for my life fully and completely, and made being a Grown Up a grand adventure where anything was possible.

I might have had a laundry list of priorities before this process began, but until I learned how to incorporate them into my day-to-day life, they were nothing more than a collection of balloons tied loosely around my wrist. Like a child at an amusement park, I might have known they were there, but they could be easily ignored as I ran around in a world filled with distractions.

The process of becoming a Grown Up involved letting go of an old self. As exciting as this was, it also had many sad elements and feelings of profound loss. In the midst of this metamorphosis, I had a vivid dream in which I was attending my own funeral. I sobbed as I saw myself lying in a white casket, and kept reaching in to grab things— a ring, a charm, other small tokens. In the dream I knew I had to say good-bye, but could not control the urge to take the tiny material objects as reminders of who I once was.

When I woke up, I knew immediately this was not a dream about my literal demise, but the death of my former self, a persona that did not fit any more. It was then that I had the bittersweet realization that a part of my life—and perhaps a certain innocence—was gone forever.

NO. 1 2 3 4 5 6 7 8½ 9 10 11

Becoming a Grown Up happened in the midst of tremendous upheaval, but it was during this time of rebirth that I discovered my strongest self and highest priorities. It was a journey of overwhelming responsibility alongside wild freedom, about opening up room in my heart for all the expansiveness and joy I wanted to create in my life. It was — and continues to be — about HOPE and JOY and Anger and Devastation, and discovering those indestructible parts of myself that have survived it all.

I began this journey by losing my way entirely, and from there, slowly but surely, I made my way back home, back to my most authentic self.

134

In any endeavor, I say,
"One day at a time,"
and I instantly Breathe easier

Because this is,
Quite Simply, the

TRUTH

I write, RUN ERRANDS, create and talk on the phone.
I take WALKS, travel, doodle, read and eat takeout Thai Food.
I listen to music, sweep our patio and BUY Flowers
at the Farmer's Market.
           Sometimes I'm totally LazY.

And it is all part of one Giant CREATIVE STEW
where the more mixed up I can make things, the
more interesting everything is... where instead of
proclaiming something does not merit the title
"Creative Act", I'll remove the
categories altogether and see
where all those tiny Bits of
inspiration and Wisdom are
HIDING today, waiting For me to
notice them. usually RIGHT under
MY Nose.

Nothing Fails

Gratitude & Acknowledgments

Ordinary Sparkling Moments came to life and made its way into the world because a lot of people supported it. If I tried to create a list of everyone who has been part of its story - friends who bought the book, wrote reviews, interviewed me on their blog, signed up to be a Book Fairy, or sent notes of gratitude - I would literally fill half of this book. Even then, it wouldn't do justice to the depth of appreciation I feel for all the love and support offered to me along the path of making this book real.

Knowing this, I decided to keep my acknowledgments brief, and offer special thanks to a small circle of supporters who showed up in extraordinary ways when I was staring at 100 boxes of inventory after the 2200 books I'd just published on my own were delivered to my house. These individuals literally bought stacks of books, held gatherings, promoted like crazy and, in one case, gave me free reign to create a bona fide *Ordinary Sparkling Moments* gallery installation in her studio.

These are friends who have stuck with me, are still in my life and continue to inspire me with their kindness, compassion and creativity. To Melissa Piccola, Blair Beggan, Jen Gray Blackburn, Jonatha Brooke, Mari Robeson, Marianne Elliott and Linda Mechanic (R.I.P.), I thank you, and I thank you and I thank you a million more times. To the magnificently long list of everyone else who comes to mind when I think about those first few months of the book's release into the world, when I sometimes wondered what I could have been thinking when I decided to write and self-publish a full-color book, *I thank you.* You made this - and have made so much more since then - possible.

I would also like to thank Tonia Jenny, who has supported, encouraged and inspired me with her honesty, enthusiasm and advocacy. Willing to listen to all of my crazy ideas and "What ifs", I appreciate her for telling me when she thinks something is a good idea as much as for when she tells me if something probably won't work. Much gratitude to Tonia and everyone at North Light Books who has believed in my work and helped create books I am incredibly proud of.

And to my family most of all, who has taught me everything I know about love and beauty and joy, and the power of dreams come true.

fw
a content + ecommerce company

Other fine North Light Books are available from your favorite bookstore, art supply store or online supplier. Visit our website at fwmedia.com.

19 18 17 16 15   5 4 3 2 1

DISTRIBUTED IN CANADA BY FRASER DIRECT
100 Armstrong Avenue
Georgetown, ON, Canada L7G 5S4
Tel: (905) 877-4411

DISTRIBUTED IN THE U.K. AND EUROPE
BY F&W MEDIA INTERNATIONAL LTD
Brunel House, Forde Close, Newton Abbot, TQ12 4PU, UK
Tel: (+44) 1626 323200, Fax: (+44) 1626 323319
Email: enquiries@fwmedia.com

DISTRIBUTED IN AUSTRALIA BY CAPRICORN LINK
P.O. Box 704, S. Windsor NSW, 2756 Australia
Tel: (02) 4560-1600; Fax: (02) 4577 5288
Email: books@capricornlink.com.au

ISBN 13: 9781440341311

Edited by Christina Richards
Designed by Elyse Schwanke
Production coordinated by Jennifer Bass

About Christine Mason Miller

Christine Mason Miller has been an author, artist and engineer of creative spaces since 1995. Her mission to inspire has provided the foundation for a body of work that has generated seven figures in retail sales through commercial illustration, licensing, gallery shows and three books. She has organized countless retreats and gatherings with some of the community's leading visionaries and change-makers - creating spaces, environments and circles that have inspired transformative healing, visionary collaborations and passionate artistic expression.

This is her second collaboration with North Light Books. Find out more about her work and adventures at **christinemasonmiller.com**.

Ideas. Instruction. Inspiration.

Receive bonus materials when you sign up for our free newsletter at
artistsnetwork.com/Newsletter_Thanks.

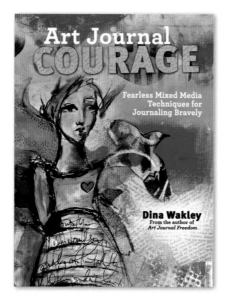

These and other fine North Light products are available at your favorite art & craft retailer, bookstore or online supplier. Visit our websites at artistsnetwork.com and artistsnetwork.tv.

Follow North Light Books for the latest news, free wallpapers, free demos and chances to win FREE BOOKS!

Get your art in print!

Visit **CreateMixedMedia.com** for up-to-date information on competitions.